Living a Transformational LIFE

Melvin Davis

ISBN 979-8-88943-383-5 (paperback)
ISBN 979-8-88943-384-2 (digital)

Christian Faith Publishing
832 Park Avenue
Meadville, PA 16335
www.christianfaithpublishing.com

Printed in the United States of America

Preface

This book has been a labor of love that represents so many things for me. First, it was directly related to a sermon that I preached at St. Andrews Baptist Church in Cleveland, Ohio, as a guest preacher on August 14, 2022. The sermon shared the same title as this book. Ironically, I was prepared to preach a different sermon for that occasion that I had prepared earlier in the week. However, I attended a leadership conference entitled "Lead Well" at my church (New Community Bible Fellowship) on August 12–August 13. The conference was amazing, and during the second day of the conference during the first breakout session, I was listening to a lecture on spiritual formation, and the lecturer was speaking on Romans 12:1–2.

During that presentation, the Holy Spirit kept whispering to my heart about living a transformational life. I wrote the topic down, and within a few minutes, I had written down the three points I would utilize during the sermon. Second, the St. Andrews congregation was very receptive to the sermon that I preached that day, including a woman who told me at the end of the service that she had been struggling with her recovery process from drugs and alcohol, but my sermon had encouraged her and helped her understand that her recovery was a process that she can achieve if she just stays committed to the steps.

Finally, a few days after the sermon, my wife said, "Why haven't you taken the numerous ideas and thoughts in your head and heart and written a book? Because I know you can do it." My wife was right, but I was making excuses about how busy I was with work and getting involved with the teen ministry at church.

Over the next two weeks, during my devotional time, the Holy Spirit started whispering the sermon title to my heart and proposed it as a book. I was surprised by the revelation but decided to be obedient to the Holy Spirit.

The purpose of this book is simply to help people live their best possible life by doing things God's way. Christians come from all walks of life, but the one thing we all have in common is that we are sinners who have been saved by God's grace because no one is worthy of salvation. However, many people who profess to be Christians often struggle with embracing the transformational power of Jesus Christ and end up settling for merely being saved rather than allowing the Holy Spirit to transform their lives. My sincere desire is that this book will help people do two things: (1) understand the importance of giving their life to Jesus Christ if they have not done so yet and (2) help people understand the importance of allowing the Holy Spirit to transform their life.

CHAPTER 1

Accepting Jesus as Savior and Lord

I'm forty-nine years old, and I have been part of the church for nearly my entire life. However, though I have always been part of the church, I did not always embrace what it truly means to be a Christian. At its most basic level, being a Christian means striving to be like Christ. Unfortunately, I look back on my college years and remember that I consistently went to church every week and enjoyed being at church, yet nothing about how I lived my life Monday through Saturday would have told anyone that I was a Christian. I did not know it at the time, but even during my undergraduate career at the Ohio State University, the Lord had his hands on me. One of the biggest lessons I have learned about God is that not even my foolishness can stop the plans he has for my life.

As I look back on the dual life I had during college of being a Christian on Sunday morning and doing whatever I wanted to do Monday through Saturday, I realize that my major issue was that I only partially embraced the message contained in God's Word. Romans 10:9 says, if you declare with your mouth Jesus is Lord and believe in your heart that God raised him from the dead, you will be saved. Romans 10:9 is often quoted as the plan for salvation, and it most definitely tells us plainly what we must do to gain salvation. However, the part that is often missed is that God is also requiring transformation from us in the text.

The text tells us that to be saved, we must make a confession that we believe in our hearts that Jesus is Lord and that God the Father raised him from the dead. If we do this, then we will be saved.

At this point, there may be some people reading this book and saying to themselves that they cannot be saved because they are focused on all the wrong things they have done in their life. If you are one of those people, then I have some good news for you. Salvation is not about merit, because if God based it on merit, then no one is going to heaven, for Romans 3:23 says, "All have sinned and fall short of the glory of God."

Yes, you read that right. According to God, not me, everyone on earth, regardless of who they are and what title they carry, may have been a sinner. None of us is better than anyone else in the sight of God. However, God does not want to leave us in our sinful state; therefore, in Romans 6:23, he declares that for the wages of sin is death, but the gift of God is eternal life through Jesus Christ our Lord. According to God, salvation is a gift, which means there is nothing that we did or ever can do to deserve or earn it. God gave it to us freely because he loves us, and his love extends to everyone regardless of what they have done if they are willing to accept him. John 3:16 says, "For God so loved the world that he gave his one and only Son that whosoever believes in him shall not perish but have eternal life." God makes it plain that he loves everyone, and if you are willing to believe in him, then he will extend salvation to you.

I believe God intentionally made access to salvation easy to help us get through the door and into the kingdom because he knows that living a Christian life requires hard work and commitment. Let's return to Romans 10:9 for a minute and examine one word in that text that has significant spiritual meaning and ramifications (yet church leaders do not emphasize it the way we should). That significant term is *Lord*. The text says we must declare that Jesus is Lord. For some strange reason, churches have glanced over teaching people, especially babies in Christ, what it means to accept Jesus as Lord.

Every Christian comes to God and accepts him as their Savior because that's the easy part since it does not require any real commitment or action on our part. But to accept Jesus as Lord means we must take the steps toward allowing Jesus to be the number one priority in our lives. The best way for me to explain it is to think of our lives as a car. Prior to accepting Jesus, we were just driving solo in the car and doing whatever we wanted to do. At some point, we feel the call of God, and we get saved. Once we get saved, we are still driving the car, but we have allowed Jesus to be in the car as a passenger; and from time to time, we accept tips from him as to what we should be doing and where we should be going. However, when we accept Jesus as Lord, it means that we have entrusted Jesus with driving the car, and we become the passengers.

It's important to understand that it is a process of moving between accepting Jesus as Savior and accepting Jesus as Lord. The thing that every Christian has in common is that we are all on the same faith journey, but we are on different parts of that journey. As a result, we must stop judging and looking down on others because we are further ahead in that journey than they are now. One of the main reasons that so many young people have turned away from the church is that too many people in church spend an inordinate amount of time judging them rather than showing them the love of God. The church is supposed to be a haven where people can come to find love, healing, support, encouragement, guidance, and empowerment. That's why Jesus declares that if he be lifted, then he will draw all men. Too many people in churches are lifting themselves rather than Jesus, which leads to repelling people instead of drawing people. The body of Christ must do a better job of showing people how to accept Jesus as Savior and providing them with what they need during their individual process so they can make the decision on their own to accept Jesus as Lord.

CHAPTER 2

Confront and Overcome Your Past

One of the biggest deterrents to Christian growth is the mistakes we have made in our past. Another thing everyone on earth has in common is that we have all engaged in some type of behavior that we regret. Unlike most Christians, Satan is on his job 24 hours a day, 7 days a week, and 365 days a year. His number one goal is to disrupt the redemptive plan of God in any way that he can. He knows that he cannot beat God in a one-on-one fight; therefore, the best way for him to disrupt the redemptive plan of God is by attacking the people of God. Before Satan decides to attack us, he is keenly aware of our wants and desires, but one of his most successful weapons is guilt.

If you do not take the time to acknowledge the mistakes you have made in your past and put forth your best effort to make amends, then those mistakes will continue to have power over you. In 12-step programs for people recovering from alcohol and/or drug addiction, the first step is acknowledging the reality that they are an addict. By acknowledging their addiction, they take back some of the power that the addiction has over them because they are on the path to recovery and restoration. Similarly, Christians must do the same thing when we come to Christ. Coming to Christ involves acknowledging that we need his help and guidance for us to become the best possible version of ourselves.

One of the many amazing things about God is that he already knows everything about us and loves us despite us; therefore, we can come to him just as we are. If we come to God just as we are and commit to doing the work of allowing him to transform us, then we will not stay the same. Second Corinthians 12:9 says, "My grace is sufficient for you, for my power is made perfect in weakness." There are two things about this scripture that have always brought me comfort. First, the apostle Paul, the person who wrote nearly two-thirds of the New Testament, still had problems. He was a spiritual giant, yet he still had to struggle with things just like the rest of us. I draw comfort from this because when I find myself struggling with various things in life, it does not mean I am a bad person or a bad Christian. Rather, it simply means that it's just my season to deal with adversity. Second, when we come to God acknowledging our struggles or weaknesses, it is at that very moment that God's power gets cemented in our life because we are having what I like to call a "get real" moment with the Lord. When you have a get-real moment with the Lord, it's when you strip away pretense, religion, and any other obstacle that is separating you from him and acknowledge that he is the only way that you will be able to find your way out.

Prior to having our get-real moment, we were bringing things to God and asking him to intervene, but we were still trying to fix it. When you bring something to God asking for his assistance, you must relinquish it. If we have our hands on it, there is no room for God to step in. But once we surrender to God, he can step in. I have found out that the simple spiritual formula that shows we have embraced living a transformational life is that we commit to doing the things that God has told us in his Word that he expects for us to do; then we trust Him to do the things that we can't do.

During my college years, I had a reputation for being hotheaded and getting into fights. I had inability to let things go so if someone did or said something that I took as an offense; then my response was typically to come out swinging. It's not something I'm proud of, but it is the reality of the person that I was at that time in my life. During my senior year of college, I went through a lot of adversity that saw me at my lowest point. My maternal grandmother and my one of my closest mentors, my fraternity brother Melvin Woodberry, had both passed away within weeks of each other, leaving a gaping hole in my life. I had gotten engaged to my high school sweetheart, but a few months later, that relationship ended as I found out that she was cheating on me. My aspiration of becoming an attorney had just been torpedoed as I was rejected by every law school that I applied to. For good measure, I was president of my chapter of my fraternity; and due to some irregularities that had happened, the university was considering penalties for my chapter and specifically against me as the chapter president. I was being threatened with criminal charges and/or potentially being kicked out of school.

During the lowest point in my life, I cried out to God late one night and promised him if he got me out of the situations that I was involved in and allowed me to graduate, I would rededicate my life to him. God responded to my prayer by telling me that I would need to make a choice of either doing things his way or continuing to do things my way. I completely surrendered to the Lord that night, and things began to change in my life. The Lord worked out all the situations I was involved in, and when I graduated from the Ohio State University on June 7, 1996, it meant the Lord had honored his promise to me, and it was time for me to do the same. Shortly after graduation, I moved back home to Cleveland, Ohio, joined a church, and began the process of rededicating my life to Christ, which meant allowing God to transform me.

At church, I joined the youth ministry as a youth worker, which gave me a platform to minister to hundreds of kids over the next twenty years; and I embraced being actively involved in Sunday school and Wednesday night Bible study. I was growing spiritually, and the seasoned saints around me could all see it. Seven years after rededicating my life to Christ, I ended my five-year period of running from God's calling on my life to preaching his Word. Until this day, many people who knew me from college are shocked to find out that I'm a preacher because of the person they remember in college, but some people take joy in trying to throw up in my face the person that I used to be. Fortunately, part of my transformation involved me confronting my past behaviors and repenting for those things to God.

During the earliest stages of me rededicating my life to Christ, I learned a scripture that really helped me process everything that I had done and move on to becoming the man the Lord was calling me to be. First Corinthians 13:11 says, "When I was a child I spoke as a child and thought as a child but when I became a man, I put away childish things." I embraced this scripture and did my best to live it out. As a result, when people from my past tried to bring me down by bringing up my extensive past, I was able to diffuse it with a smile by saying, "Yes, I remember doing all those things, but I have not been that person for a very long time."

I shared that part of my journey to encourage each of you to come to Christ just as you are. Allow him to begin the process of transforming you. Confront your past. You are more than the sum of the mistakes that you have made in your life. If you have already accepted Christ and you find yourself in situations where Satan is whispering in your ear that you are not worthy to minister to people because of the things you have done in your life, you can put him in his place and keep serving the Lord. After all, if I was able to do it, it means that anyone can do it because the only thing special about me is that the Spirit of God resides inside me. God is waiting on you to surrender to him so he can transform you. That's why he declares in 2 Corinthians 5:17 that if any man be in Christ, he is a new creation; old things are passed away and all things become new. I challenge you to make that new start in your life by surrendering to God.

You Must Be All In

One of the most significant things we must do to start living a transformational life is to make the decision that our spiritual life is lacking something right now. This is hard to do because we can become distracted with doing church work rather than doing the work of the church. Church work is all the tasks that we participate in at the physical church building such as being an usher, singing in the choir, serving as a deacon or in the pulpit ministry, being Sunday school superintendent or director of Vacation Bible School, just to name a few. On the other hand, doing the work of the church requires us to move beyond the four walls of the church. The best way to move beyond the walls of the church is by embracing the Great Commission.

> Then the eleven disciples went to Galilee to the Mountain where Jesus had told them to go. When they saw him, they worshipped him, but some doubted. Then Jesus came to them and said, "All authority in heaven and an on earth has been given to me. Therefore go and make disciples of all nations, baptizing them in the name of the Father and of the Son and of the Holy Spirit, and teaching them to obey everything I have commanded you. And surely I am with you always, to the very end of the age. (Matthew 28:16–20)

Every time the Bible records Jesus speaking, we should pay close attention because there is always purpose behind his words. However, the Great Commission has added importance because these words are coming from the resurrected Jesus prior to his ascension back to heaven. Furthermore, Jesus is issuing marching orders intended for all Christians for all time.

An examination of the text reveals that Jesus is clearly placing the emphasis on activities being done outside the four walls of the church rather than being confined inside the church. The first thing Jesus says is "Go." He is commanding the disciples to leave their respective comfort zones (i.e., Jerusalem) and travel to other places to introduce the Gospel and, more importantly, to model the Gospel. Let me be clear: I'm not suggesting that every Christian has a spiritual mandate to go out and preach. However, I do believe every Christian has the responsibility to model the Gospel in every area of their life.

Even though I've been raised in the church, it wasn't until my late twenties that I realized that the way I lived my life, especially my interactions with people, could go further in spreading the Gospel than any of the service that I routinely performed at my local fellowship. The reason for this is that we have seen a proliferation of the unchurched generation, which simply means people who have little to no exposure to the church or the Bible. As a result, the only sermon that many people in the unchurched generation will experience is their interactions with Christians because how we treat people is supposed to reflect the love of God.

The Bible says it this way:

> In the same way, faith by itself, if it is unaccompanied by action, is dead. But someone will say, you have faith; I have deeds. Show me your faith without deeds, and I will show you my faith by what I do. (James 2:17–18)

Far too often, the church—by this I mean the universal church, not any specific local fellowship—is guilty of limiting this conversation to the ministries that we are involved in at our local fellowships.

Yes, it is important for Christians to be actively involved in at least one ministry at their local fellowship, but if the things we are learning at church and through the study of God's Word are not carried into our personal lives outside the church, then our faith should be considered dead.

The first eulogy I ever gave as a preacher occurred in 2017, and it was for Jacqueline Barnes. She is the mother of Ricardo Barnes, who has been one of my best friends since we were twelve years old, and his mom was certainly like another mom to me. She was an amazing woman who was soft-spoken and always had a kind word for everyone. In all the years that I was privileged to have her be part of my life, I had never heard her quote a scripture. She went to church, but she didn't hold any special titles at church. However, her lasting impact on this side of time is how she treated people. In her interactions with people, she always showed the love of Jesus Christ even to those who, by their very actions, were not loveable. I miss her dearly, but I'm so grateful that I had the opportunity to witness firsthand how God expects Christians to treat people because Mama Jackie modeled it for me every day of her life.

If we are to begin living a transformational life, then it means we can no longer straddle the fence. We have got to decide to be all in for Jesus Christ. Being all in doesn't mean we have to go around beating people over the head with the Bible or that we can no longer participate in secular activities. However, it does mean embracing a desire to see the world and people through the eyes and heart of Jesus as expressed in the Bible. Change will not come in our lives until we unambiguously make the decision that we want to change for the better.

Scripture reflects this mindset this way:

> Therefore, I urge you, brothers, in view of god's
> mercy, to offer your bodies as living sacrifices,
> holy and pleasing to God, this is your spiritual
> act of worship. (Romans 12:1)

Presenting our bodies as living sacrifices to God simply means we are deciding to embrace living for him. When we first come to Christ, we are accepted into the family of God through salvation because we have accepted Jesus as our Savior. This is an incredible and necessary first step. However, it is only the beginning of a spiritual journey in which we are supposed to grow in our understanding of God and how to live as his people. The next step that so many people who profess to be Christians struggle to make that is reflected in Romans 12:1 is embracing Jesus as Lord, which we covered in chapter 1.

CHAPTER 4

Change the Way You Think

The main reason so many Christians struggle with living a transformational life is that they put most of their effort into trying to address behavior rather than trying to change the way they think. When we put our energy into changing behavior without changing how we think, the change is only temporary.

> Do not conform any longer to the pattern of
> this world, but be transformed by the renewing
> of your mind. Then you will be able to test and
> approve what God's will is his good, pleasing and
> perfect will. (Romans 12:2)

When we come to Christ, we all come to him with years of baggage from a life spent doing things that are often completely contrary to the will of God but perfectly acceptable and natural in the secular world. We have learned bad habits, and we must embrace doing things differently once we become Christians. Romans 12:2 expressly states that transformation occurs when we change the way we think. However, changing a lifetime of bad habits and decision-making does not occur overnight; rather, it is a process.

The process of changing the way we think begins with us embracing God's Word, will for our lives, and doing things his way. This is often difficult because society has conditioned us to believe and embrace certain things. A good example occurs in Exodus 18:7–27. Jethro, father-in-law to Moses, came to visit him. During the visit, Jethro witnessed Moses serving as a judge to all the people from morning until evening. Jethro told Moses that he needed help to judge the people, so he should appoint capable, trustworthy men who can serve as judges, and the difficult cases can be brought to Moses. Thankfully, Moses listened to his father-in-law and implemented all his suggestions.

Today and even in biblical times, men were socialized to believing that they are supposed to always handle everything on their own and project strength. However, Jethro showed wisdom in his suggestion to Moses, and Moses listened to his wise counsel. The system of judges that Moses set in motion foreshadowed a similar system that we would see the early church embrace when it created what we now know as deacons.

It's a sad commentary and indictment on us as men that so many of us try to do everything on our own because we falsely believe that asking for help makes us less of a man. When we look to Jesus as our example, we see evidence that immediately refutes this notion. Jesus is God the Son, which means he is all powerful; yet when he began his public ministry, the first thing he did was choose twelve people to assist him. If Jesus sought out help, then men need to be secure enough in our masculinity to seek out help when we need it.

Though, we are often our own worst enemy when it comes to changing the way we think. Another major issue is that we often allow ourselves to become imprisoned to our past and to other people's expectations of us due to our past. However, the Bible declares that where the spirit of the Lord is, there is liberty. Liberty means freedom from arbitrary control. God has given us liberty when we accepted Christ, but we still must make a conscious decision to walk in the liberty that has been granted to us. However, we need to learn how to do it, and scripture gives us some key points.

> Therefore, if anyone is in Christ, the new creation has come: The old has gone, the new is here. (2 Corinthians 5:17)

The great news about becoming a Christian is that God sees us as a new creation now. All of our sins have now been covered by the blood that Jesus shed on Calvary. We can't change the reality of the sinful things we have done, but God has given us a new opportunity to turn away from those things and toward him. However, let me warn you that when you start making changes in your life as you try to live for Christ, some people in your life will constantly try to hold your past over your head. Please don't waste your time and energy on arguing with people about you no longer being the same person. Instead, the best approach is for you to keep walking in the path that God has placed you on because action is always better than words.

Furthermore, some people are so closed-minded that they will never accept the changes that you are making in your life because they are not at a point where they are ready to make any changes in their life. As a result, your spiritual progress shines a light on the reality that they are choosing to remain in darkness.

CHAPTER 5

Expect and Endure Adversity

We are living in times where many televangelists have gotten rich by convincing Christians to believe things that are untrue and, in many cases, completely contrary to the Bible. These televangelists have been preying on vulnerable people because they know numerous people are looking for someone to give them a simple recipe or road map to follow, and if they follow that road map or recipe, they will be successful and live a good life. Televangelists have used enticing catchphrases such as "name it and claim it" or "call it and haul it" to set up the false expectations that believers can avoid the troubles of life with positive thinking and how much money they contribute to a particular church.

Televangelists understand that sermons that make people feel good will motivate them to give you their money. As a result, they tell people what they want to hear rather than the principles that God has provided to us in his Word. The latter is like taking medicine or eating vegetables; meaning, it may not taste very good, but it's good for you and will help you heal and grow.

I hate to be the bearer of bad news, but there is nowhere in Scripture where God promised us that we would be free from problems. Contrary to what many have been led to believe, just because you faithfully attend church each week, pay your tithes, and serve in a ministry at church, that does not guarantee you that you will be immune from the problems of life. I heard a preacher many years ago say that there are three stages of life: (1) you are in a storm, (2) headed for a storm, or (3) coming out of a storm. These stages are also cyclical, which means they are never ending if we are living on this side of time. Consequently, the question is not whether we will find ourselves in a storm but what we will do once we find ourselves during the storm. Let's look at one of the biblical stories using the storm imagery to illustrate this principle.

> That day when evening came, he said to his disciples, "Let us go over to the other side." Leaving the crowd behind, they took him along, just as he was in the boat. There were also other boats with him. A furious squall came up, and the waves broke over the boat, so that it was nearly swamped. Jesus was in the stern sleeping on a cushion. The disciples woke and said to him, "Teacher, don't you care if we drown?" He got up, rebuked the wind and said to the waves, "Quiet! Be still!" Then the wind died down and it was completely calm. He said to his disciples, "Why are you so afraid? Do you still have no faith?" They were terrified and asked each other, "Who is this? Even the wind and the waves obey him!" (Mark 4:35–41)

There are a few points I want to examine in the text that can help our understanding about the place that adversity or storms play in the life of a Christian. First, the central thing that every Christian must learn to do is to trust Jesus. We should trust Jesus because he has proven repeatedly that he is trustworthy by keeping his promises. In verse 35, Jesus makes a statement ("Let us go over to the other side"), but this statement also contains a promise. Implicit in the statement is the promise from Jesus that they will make it to the other side. Please take a few moments and reflect on this point. Adversity is always waiting on us, and Satan himself is always looking for an opportunity to disrupt God's redemptive plan for our lives. However, regardless of what storm or adversity we experience, just as Jesus promised the disciples that they would make it to the other side, he does the same thing for you and me.

At the end of the day, it comes down to one simple point: do you trust Jesus? If the answer to that question is yes, then it means you can persevere when you find yourself facing the storms of life. If the answer to that question is no, then it means you have a much bigger problem. It means that you are probably at a point in your life where you are still living off and standing upon someone else's faith.

The overwhelming majority of Christians came to know Christ because of someone else in their life such as a parent, aunt, uncle, cousin, grandparent, neighbor, or friend. Over the course of our lives, we have had strong Christians praying for us even when we didn't have enough sense to pray for ourselves. I remember as a kid my grandmother used to tell me that God was going to use me one day. I didn't know what Grandma was talking about back then, but I did like the sound of God using me.

I was raised in the church and always enjoyed going to church, but my grandmother and so many other "seasoned" saints in my life had a level of faith that I simply couldn't understand. I couldn't understand it because I hadn't lived long enough to go through some ordeals and come out on the other side knowing that it was God that brought me through that situation. When you lack that type of experience in your life, it's hard to trust God because you don't have anything to base it on. As a result, the only way that I survived the times when I was young and dumb is that those seasoned saints like my grandmother were standing in the gap praying for me and asking the Lord to intercede on my behalf. I'm grateful for those seasoned saints, but I'm at a point in my life where I don't need to stand on my grandmother's faith anymore because I know Jesus for myself. I have experienced him bring me through situations where I know it was God.

At this stage in the text and in the disciples' spiritual journey, they simply hadn't built up a foundation of trust in Jesus despite all the miracles they had already seen him perform. When we examine the text, we also see our second point. Storms will come into all our lives, and there is simply nothing we can do about it. Also, you don't need to do anything wrong to have storms in your life because the Bible clearly tells us that it rains on the just as well as the unjust.

In the text, the disciples found themselves facing a storm so severe that the waves were crashing against the boat. However, this was no ordinary storm because of the response of the disciples. Peter, James, and John were all professional fishermen, which means they had plenty of experience sailing those waters and what to do when a storm arose. Unfortunately, this storm was so severe that their professional training didn't help them navigate the situation at all, which led to the disciples becoming terrified.

The response of the disciples is typical of many people. When we have training or education, our tendency is to rely on our training and education while ignoring God. However, when our training and education fails us, as a last-ditch effort, we take the situation to God, asking for his help. I said earlier that the main issue is that the disciples had a trust problem. Remember, Jesus promised that they were going to make it to the other side. If the disciples trusted in him, then it would not matter how severe the storm was—they would simply trust Jesus.

The final point about storms is that they are temporary and bend to the will of God. Many times, when the storm begins raging in our life, it appears to be so severe that we can feel completely powerless and helpless. It's in these situations that we are tempted to give up. However, it's during these times that we need to remind ourselves of who we are and whose we are. We are the children of God, so we have a special relationship with God. Hebrews 4:16 says, "Let us approach God's throne of grace with confidence, so that we may receive mercy and find grace to help us in our time of need."

Some people have an issue going before God because they focus on feeling unworthy. It's true that we can never be worthy of God's love because Scripture tells us that all have sinned and come short of the glory of God. Fortunately, God's mercy and grace covers all our flaws and sins. God's mercy grants us forgiveness or withholds punishment, but God's grace is his unmerited gift of divine favor toward us. Simply put, there is nothing that we can ever do to earn God's grace because he has chosen to give it to us freely because he loves us. As a result, when the storm is raging in our life, we can appeal to God and obtain grace and mercy.

CHAPTER 6

Launching Out Into the Deep

I have been involved in church leadership for approximately twenty years. During this period, I have experienced numerous types of leadership styles and watched numerous leaders. As a result, I have had the opportunity to see the difference between good leadership and bad leadership. No one has a goal of becoming a bad leader, especially in the church setting. Unfortunately, we tend to practice what we see rather than seek out authentic biblical leadership. In my opinion, the most important aspect of biblical leadership is our willingness to launch out into the deep. Let's examine a biblical story about the calling of the first disciples for us to explore this concept.

> One day as Jesus was standing by the Lake of Gennesaret, with the people crowding around him and listening to the word of God, he saw at the water's edge two boats, left there by the fishermen, who were washing their nets. He got into one of the boats, the one belonging to Simon, and asked him to put out a little from shore. Then he sat down and taught the people from the boat.
>
> When he had finished speaking, he said to Simon, "Put out into deep water, and let down the nets for a catch."

Simon answered, "Master, we've worked hard all night and haven't caught anything. But because you say so, I will let down the nets."

When they had done so, they caught such a large number of fish that their nets began to break. So they signaled their partners in the other boat to come and help them, and they came and filled both boats so full that they began to sink.

When Simon Peter saw this, he fell at Jesus' knees and said, "Go away from me Lord; I am a sinful man!" For he and all his companions were astonished at the catch of fish they had taken and so were James and John, the sons of Zebedee, Simon's partners.

Then Jesus said to Simon, "Don't be afraid; from now on you will catch men." So they pulled their boats up on shore, left everything and followed him. (Luke 5:1–11)

One of the first principles of biblical leadership is a willingness to be obedient to Jesus. In the text, Jesus comes to Peter after Peter has had a long night of fruitless fishing as he and his business partners caught no fish. Jesus turns Peter's boat into a pulpit as he teaches the people from it; but after he finishes teaching the people, he tells Peter to go out into the deep water so he can catch some fish. This command from Jesus is meant to determine whether Peter is willing to be obedient to Jesus. To fully understand this situation, we must explore who Peter and Jesus are at this point and where these events are taking place

Both Jesus and Peter grew up in the small towns of Galilee. One of the things that is unique to small towns is that everyone knows one another and typically knows one another's business. As a result, Peter is fully aware that Jesus is a carpenter by trade, which means here is a carpenter trying to tell a professional fisherman how and where to fish. It would be completely understandable for Peter to dismiss Jesus at this point because his training and experience says he knows more about fishing than any carpenter. However, Peter has a front-row seat to the teachings of Jesus and understands that he is a master teacher who is entitled to respect and deference. As a result, he is obedient and goes out to the deep part of the water just as Jesus has asked him to do.

One of the things that often sidetracks Christians from living a transformational life is that we are more obedient to our education and skills than we are the Word of God. It is something that I have certainly wrestled with in ministry as I have had many moments like Peter whereby, ultimately, I do what God is telling me to do, but not before I let him know how I feel about what he is asking me to do. It's amazing to me that the creation has the unmitigated gall or temerity to ever think they know more than the Creator. Education and experience are very good things to have and strive for, but they must be subjugated to God just like everything else. Peter didn't fully understand at this point that Jesus was the Son of God, but he was impressed enough with the teachings and miracles he had seen him do that he was willing to defer to Jesus.

Another important aspect of biblical leadership is we must be willing to go out into deep water. In the text, Jesus is literally talking about deep water, but the spiritual implications are abundant here. Many people who profess to be Christians never move beyond the shallow water in their relationship with God and other people. If you remain in the shallow water, then you will never experience any real adversity because you can always just stand up and walk away. However, God expects us to become deep-water people who can move beyond our comfort zones and allow God to use us in new ways.

One of the things I have always found interesting about biblical stories in which God calls someone into service is that in the overwhelming majority of situations, God calls someone out of something and into something else. The simple rationale for this pattern is that God knows that if he calls us to do something that we already have education or experience doing, then we are much more likely to rely solely on our education and experiences. On the other hand, if God calls us into a brand-new area, then the only way we can be successful is by depending upon Him.

A final aspect of biblical leadership is a willingness to be fully committed to Jesus. In the text, Peter lets down the nets in the place where Jesus commands; and although he and his partners has unsuccessfully fished that entire area all night now, he catches so many fish that he must call his business partners to help him catch them all. Peter's response to this phenomenal miracle was relinquishing everything to follow Jesus. When God does something amazing in your life that you know beyond a shadow of a doubt can only be attributable to him, then the appropriate response from us should be committing ourselves to God just as Peter, James, John, and Andrew did.

When you commit yourself to God, it means embracing a new way of thinking and a new way of doing things. Doing things God's way can be confusing and sometimes downright terrifying because it often goes completely against the things you have thought and done your entire life. However, as Christians, we must become comfortable with being uncomfortable for God. I'm at a point in my life where I have accepted that it is not a requirement that I understand or agree with the things God is asking me to do because this is not a democracy. It's a theocracy with God as the head, and when he speaks, I simply need to listen and obey.

CHAPTER 7

Use Wisdom in Choosing Your Friends

It's important to use wisdom in determining the people that you allow in your life as friends. As Christians, we should strive to ensure that the people who are in our inner circle are like-minded and have our best interests at heart. If you surround yourself with naysayers, doubters, and negative people in your circle of friends, it makes it more difficult for you to stay on the path of living a transformational life as these types of people are unlikely to be supportive of the changes you desire to make in your life.

Unfortunately, many Christians are guilty of using incredibly poor judgment in determining the people they call friends. Typically, the biggest mistake is that we fail to heed the advice that was offered by the famous poet Maya Angelou when she said, "When people show you who they are, believe them the first time." We accept people into our lives as friends, and when they have a demonstrated track record of doing things to show us that they are the antithesis of a friend, rather than accept the truth, we make excuses for their actions or behaviors. Contrary to popular belief, knowing someone for a long time does not mean we should view that person as a friend. We must have higher standards than merely the length of time we have known a person. Let's look at a biblical example of friendship and the impact it can have on our lives.

A few days later, when Jesus again entered Capernaum, the people heard that he had come home. They gathered in such large numbers that there was no room left, not even outside the door, and he preached the word to them. Some men came, bringing to him a paralyzed man, carried by four of them. Since they could not get him to Jesus because of the crowd, they made an opening in the roof above Jesus by digging through it and then lowered the mat the man was lying on.

When Jesus saw their faith, he said to the paralyzed man, "Son, your sins are forgiven."

Now some teachers of the law were sitting there, thinking to themselves, "Why does this fellow talk like that? He's blaspheming! Who can forgive sins but God alone?"

Immediately Jesus knew in his spirit that this was what they were thinking in their hearts, and he said to them, "Why are you thinking these things? Which is easier: to say to this paralyzed man, 'Your sins are forgiven,' or to say, 'Get up, take your mat and walk'? But I want you to know that the Son of Man has authority on earth to forgive sins." So he said to the man, "I tell you, get up, take your mat and go home."

He got up, took his mat and walked out in full view of them all. This amazed everyone and they praised God, saying, "We have never seen anything like this!" (Mark 2:1–5)

In the text, four men are carrying a paralyzed man. I find it very interesting that the Bible does not label the men as friends of the paralyzed man, yet their actions are most definitely that of a friend. The first attribute we learn of friends is that they are compassionate. To be compassionate, one must show genuine concern for the well-being of others. The paralyzed man is unable to take care of himself, and depending upon the nature of his injuries, he could even be in pain. The four men took it upon themselves to help improve the man's situation. They did not have the power to heal him themselves, but when they heard that Jesus was in town, they carried the paralyzed man to Jesus because they had likely heard stories of him performing miracles, which included healing people.

The second attribute of friendship is trustworthiness. In the text, the four men arrived at the place where Jesus was, but it was so crowded with people who were there to either see Jesus, hear him teach, or be healed by him that there was no way for the four men to get the paralyzed man to Jesus. In this situation, no one would blame these men for giving up and just conceding that they gave it their best shot. Amazingly, the four men came up with an action plan that involved climbing the building to get to the roof, making a hole in the roof, and lowering the paralyzed man down to Jesus. The perseverance and faith of the four men is downright amazing, but this is a time where I want you to use your imagination to visualize how this situation unfolded.

At some point, the four men likely explained to the paralyzed man their action plan. The paralyzed man would likely be "dead weight," which means he would be completely unable to assist them in carrying him up the building. In other words, the paralyzed man had to trust the four men completely that they could perform this task without dropping him either while going up the building or while lowering him down to Jesus. Being trustworthy should be one of the most important attributes of friendship because when that person says they are going to do something, you must be able to trust that they are going to do what they say they are going to do. On the other hand, when a person's actions consistently show that they are untrustworthy, then you should not identify that person as one of your friends.

The final attribute of friendship is that they are willing to endure hard times or adversity. The paralyzed man had likely been suffering for quite some time, and it's even possible that maybe he had given up. Fortunately, his four friends cared about him enough that they were willing to go through extreme measures to get him to the only person who could heal him. One of the simple truths in life is that you find out who you friends truly are during times of adversity. Friends are the ones whom you can count on to be there for you during the tough times.

If you have people in your life that you identify as friends but they are missing one or more of the three attributes we just discussed, then it's time for you to reevaluate that relationship. You must ask yourself why you are still holding on to this person as a friend despite the reality that their actions have proven that they are not a friend.

CHAPTER 8

Understanding the Importance of Forgiveness

The willingness to forgive is at the center of the Christian faith. The story of Adam and Eve is typically the first biblical story that kids learn in church because their sin in the Garden of Eden ushered sin into the world and changed the course of human history. Let's do a quick refresher course on the story so we can see the role that forgiveness played.

> Now the serpent was more crafty than any of the wild animals the Lord God had made. He said to the woman, "Did God really say, 'You must not eat from any tree in the garden'?"
>
> The woman said to the serpent, "We may eat fruit from the trees in the garden, but God did say, 'You must not eat fruit from the tree that is in the middle of the garden, and you must not touch it, or you will die.'"
>
> "You will not certainly die," the serpent said to the woman. "For God knows that when you eat from it your eyes will be opened, and you will be like God, knowing good and evil."
>
> When the woman saw that the fruit of the tree was good for food and pleasing to the eye, and also desirable for gaining wisdom, she

took some and ate it. She also gave some to her husband, who was with her, and he ate it. Then the eyes of both of them were opened, and they realized they were naked; so they sewed fig leaves together and made coverings for themselves.

Then the man and his wife heard the sound of the Lord God as he was walking in the garden in the cool of the day, and they hid from the Lord God among the trees of the garden. But the Lord God called to the man, "Where are you?"

He answered, "I heard you in the garden, and I was afraid because I was naked; so I hid."

And he said, "Who told you that you were naked? Have you eaten from the tree that I commanded you not to eat from?"

The man said, "The woman you put here with me—she gave me some fruit from the tree, and I ate it."

Then the Lord God said to the woman, "What is this you have done?"

The woman said, "The serpent deceived me, and I ate."

So the Lord God said to the serpent, "Because you have done this, "Cursed are you above all livestock and all wild animals! You will crawl on your belly and you will eat dust all the days of your life. And I will put enmity between you and the woman, and between your offspring and hers; he will crush your head, and you will strike his heel."

To the woman he said, "I will make your pains in childbearing very severe; with painful labor you will give birth to children. Your desire will be for your husband, and he will rule over you."

To Adam he said, "Because you listened to your wife and ate fruit from the tree about which I commanded you, 'You must not eat from it,' "Cursed is the ground because of you; through painful toil you will eat food from it all the days of your life. It will produce thorns and thistles for you, and you will eat the plants of the field. By the sweat of your brow you will eat your food until you return to the ground, since from it you were taken; for dust you are and to dust you will return." (Genesis 3:1–19)

One of the first notable things from this story is the response of God to the reality that the disobedience of Adam and Eve had brought sin into the world, which would have long-lasting consequences not just on humanity but on animals and even the earth itself. God came walking in the garden and directed his line of questioning to Adam first, not Eve. This is very significant because Eve was the person who sinned first by eating the fruit, then gave it to Adam, who quickly followed suit. However, God was not concerned about the chronological order of the sin; rather, he held Adam responsible because Adam was the person whom he placed in charge, not Eve. Remember, Adam was created first, and it was Adam who was given dominion over everything, including giving names to the animals, and it was Adam who first designated female as woman.

Furthermore, though the church has often vilified Eve for centuries for eating the forbidden fruit, the reality of the situation is that Adam was present during Eve's encounter with the serpent, which means he should have spoken up or taken some action to ensure that neither he nor Eve ate the fruit. Instead, Adam cared more about pleasing his wife than he did pleasing God.

During this accountability moment, God asked Adam where he was. Now of God's inquiry, Adam and Eve were hiding, yet God's question had nothing to do with Adam's physical location since he is omnipotent (all powerful), omniscient (all knowing), and omnipresent (everywhere), which means he already knew their physical location. God's question to Adam was about where Adam stood in his relationship with God since he listened to his wife instead of God. Unfortunately, both Adam and Eve played the blame game. Adam blamed Eve for giving him the forbidden fruit, and he had the temerity to blame God for giving him Eve as his wife. Eve attempted to avoid accountability as well as she blamed the serpent for tricking her. As I will talk about in a moment when we discuss the Matthew 18 principle, one of the important parts of forgiveness is bringing the sin or offense to the person's attention, which gives the offender the opportunity to take responsibility for their action and repent. Unfortunately, Adam and Eve sought to avoid responsibility for their actions just like many contemporary Christians do today when confronted with sin.

Clearly, God is disappointed with his children's sin, but in my opinion, I think he was even more hurt that neither of them were willing to take responsibility for their actions. Now, it was time for God to help Adam and Eve understand the seriousness of their actions. He did this by issuing a series of punishments. For the serpent, God cursed him so that he would crawl on his belly for the rest of his life, and he put enmity between the serpent and humanity. This part of the text implies that prior to the serpent's role in Adam and Eve's sin, the serpent walked upright rather than crawling on its belly as it does today. Also, God put enmity (a sense of hostility or opposition toward someone or something) between the serpent and humanity, which accounts for why so many people today have a natural mistrust or fear of snakes.

The most significant pronouncement of God is when he says, "The offspring of the woman will crush the serpent." This statement is incredibly important for two reasons. First, it's the first biblical reference to the coming of Jesus, for it is Jesus who will ultimately be responsible for destroying Satan. Second, Adam and Eve's sin caused a spiritual separation between God and humanity; yet as he dealt with their sin, God already put a plan in place to restore humanity back to himself, which is accomplished hundreds of years later through the birth, death, and resurrection of Jesus. Simply put, instead of God holding a grudge against humanity for committing sin and not even having enough sense to apologize, God shows a willingness to forgive by creating his redemptive plan.

Forgiveness is powerful, yet most people don't fully understand forgiveness. Most people have heard someone say some version of the statement, "I forgive people, but I don't forget." This statement is the antithesis of forgiveness because it implies that we will always hold the person's actions against them rather than giving them the opportunity to repent and prove to us that they have changed by their actions. From a biblical perspective, forgiveness means to treat someone as if the offense never occurred. According to this definition, I feel confident in saying most people who profess to be Christians have either only forgiven an extremely small number of people and, in many cases, have not forgiven anyone at all.

I grew up in a family where holding grudges is normal. My mom's side of the family is huge as she has five brothers and five sisters. Unfortunately, a huge trend in the Davis family is our willingness to hold grudges against people who we think have wronged us. I have family members who haven't spoken to each other in so many years that they do not even remember why they are mad. When I was growing up, it was normal for my mom to get mad at my dad for something he did or, for that matter, didn't do and not speak to him for a month. When she was mad at my dad, not only did she give him the silent treatment, but she also didn't do anything for him such as cooking or washing his clothes. At that point in my life, my dad had zero ability to cook or wash clothes; therefore, my mom cutting him off had a serious impact on him. I used to feel bad for him because my mom would cook just enough dinner for me and her to eat, which meant he had to go out and either buy fast food or go eat at his sister's house. I know this sounds ridiculous and hard to believe, but I'm trying to paint the picture for you of how difficult it was for me to learn how to forgive people because I didn't have many examples of it in my personal life.

Another issue that people have with forgiveness is that they mistakenly believe that forgiving people makes you weak. On the contrary, it takes strength and character to forgive people; but more importantly, forgiveness is for you, not the other person. If you are feeling good, then a person walks in the room and their mere presence changes your entire atmosphere, it means that person has power over you. Once I learned this principle, it became easier for me to forgive people. When you forgive people for the hurt that they have caused you, you retake your power from that person, and you can move on with your life. In some cases, you may need to confront that person to tell them how they hurt you, or in other situations, you can write your feelings down in a letter to either send to that person or just to get it all out. Both situations allow you to say what you need to say to that person, forgive them, and most importantly, move on with your life.

Jesus often addressed the importance of forgiveness because he knows its power. I won't address every biblical text about forgiveness, but I do want to take a few minutes to explore what is commonly referred to as the Matthew 18 principle because Jesus lays out some practical things as it relates to forgiveness.

> "If your brother or sister sins, go and point out their fault, just between the two of you. If they listen to you, you have won them over. But if they will not listen, take one or two others along, so that 'every matter may be established by the testimony of two or three witnesses.' If they still refuse to listen, tell it to the church; and if they refuse to listen even to the church, treat them as you would a pagan or a tax collector. "Truly I tell you, whatever you bind on earth will be bound in heaven, and whatever you loose on earth will be loosed in heaven. "Again, truly I tell you that if two of you on earth agree about anything they ask for, it will be done for them by my Father in heaven. For where two or three gather in my name, there am I with them." (Matthew 18:15–20)

One of the first points in this principle is that Jesus puts the responsibility of reconciliation on the person who has been offended rather than on the offender. When I first read this as an adult in my early twenties, it did not make any sense to me. In my mind, the person who is in the wrong should have the responsibility to go to the person whom they have wronged to try to make amends. However, as I matured in Christ, I began to look at the text differently and realized why Jesus put the onus on the person who has been offended. As I looked back over my own life, I realized there were many times where either I offended someone or someone offended me, but neither of us knew that we had offended the other person. By requiring the person who has been offended to go to the offender and bring to their attention that their actions and/or comments have offended them and explain why you are offended, it puts the person on notice that an offense has occurred. Once the person has been notified of an offense, now the door has been firmly opened for reconciliation. The offender has two options at their disposal: (1) take responsibility for their actions or comments or (2) refuse to accept responsibility.

Contrary to popular opinion, getting angry or mad is not a sin. The sin lies in staying mad. Christians are required to seek out reconciliation which, is why Ephesians 4:26 says, "In your anger do not sin: Do not let the sun go down while you are still angry." The more time we allow to elapse before seeking out reconciliation, the greater likelihood there is of the situation leading to anger, resentment, and potential misunderstandings.

The second point in the principle is that the initial discussion on the matter should be solely between the offended and the offender. One of the quickest ways for situations to be blown out of proportion is when the person who has been offended seeks out an audience for their grievance. Typically, this is done to have one or more people take the offended person's side. If the offended person seeks out the offender with an audience who is already firmly on the offended person's side, there is the potential for the situation to needlessly escalate because the offender can become defensive rather than trying to understand the offended person's grievance. If the initial discussion on the matter is only between the offender and the person who has been offended, there is a better chance of it being resolved amicably and quickly.

The third point in the principle prepares for the possibility that the offender will refuse to accept responsibility for their actions and/or comments. If that situation occurs, then the next step is for the offended person to go and get another person to come back to serve as a witness that the offended person has put forth an honest effort to try to resolve the matter. In biblical times, two or more people were often required to establish the veracity of a statement. The goal of this approach is that the neutral third party will help the offender and offended person reconcile.

The fourth point in the principle says, if the person is unwilling to listen to the third party, then the matter should be brought before the church. If the offender is unwilling to listen to the church, then the offender is to be cast out until they are prepared to listen. Many have interrupted this point to favor excommunication or kicking someone out of the church. However, it is important to understand that casting the person out is meant to be a temporary disciplinary technique because reconciliation is still the goal. However, we cannot force anyone into reconciliation; they must be convicted to do it on their own, or it will not be genuine.

Forgiveness is one of the key tenets of Christianity. God forgives us because he loves us, not because we deserve forgiveness. Consequently, we have an obligation to forgive others as well. We cannot live a transformational life if we are walking around holding grudges against people or are completely unwilling to forgive them.

CHAPTER 9

Overcoming a Faith Crisis

A faith crisis is a point in time where the adversity or tension we are dealing with temporarily outruns our faith. I hate to be the bearer of bad news, but I am going to let you in on a secret: if you have never experienced a faith crisis in your life, then just keep on living because life has a way of dishing out the perfect set of circumstances to set the stage for us to have a faith crisis. I can see the wheels turning in your head as you are reading this now, and you are thinking about how strong your faith is, the spiritual responsibilities you have earned at your church, the people who look up to you, or the many times you have overcome obstacles in your life. I understand that all those things may very well be true, but they do not make you immune to a faith crisis.

In my opinion, the reason that super Christians (this is my term for people who act as though it is not possible for them to ever doubt God or to temporarily turn their backs on God) will refuse to believe they could ever have a faith crisis is the bad theology that often surrounds a faith crisis. Many Christians have been led to believe that questioning or doubting God means that you are a bad Christian, and being a bad Christian can have the eternal consequence of you losing your salvation. I disagree with this line of reasoning, and more importantly, the Bible gives us numerous examples of legendary spiritual giants who experienced a faith crisis at some point in their life.

Abraham is referred to as the father of the faithful, yet he experienced a faith crisis as well. In Genesis 20:1–17, we learn that when King Abimelech of Gerar was interested in making Sarah one of his wives, he approached Abraham about his relationship to Sarah. Abraham believed that if he told the truth that she was his wife, then he would be killed so King Abimelech could simply take his wife. As a result, he told the king that she was his sister, so Abimelech brought her to his house. Abraham's deception was based solely on the fact that he did not trust God to protect him in that situation, in a land where he did not believe there was any fear of the Lord.

Fortunately, Abimelech did not touch Sarah because, in a dream, the Lord told him several key things: (1) Sarah was Abraham's wife; (2) Abraham was a prophet; (3) if Abimelech did not return her to Abraham, the Lord would kill him and his entire household; (4) the Lord understood that Abimelech did not consciously take another man's wife, which is why He kept Abimelech from touching her; and (5) after returning Sarah, Abraham will pray for him, which will allow Abimelech to live.

Beyond a shadow of a doubt, Abraham was completely wrong in this situation, and his faith crisis had the potential of causing someone to lose their life. Thankfully, God extended his grace and mercy to Abimelech and Abraham to make the situation right. This story is a spiritual failure on the part of Abraham, but his spiritual failure in this scenario did not prevent God from honoring his promise to make Abraham the father of many nations and blessing the entire world through Abraham. Similarly, when you and I have a faith crisis, it does not brand us with a scarlet letter or in any way mean that God can no longer use us as part of his redemptive plan. Furthermore, our sin does not define who we are or what we can accomplish. However, it is important for us to learn how to overcome a faith crisis and to learn from it. Thankfully, the Bible gives us a great story that shows how to overcome a faith crisis, so let's look at the story:

> Now Ahab told Jezebel everything Elijah had done and how he had killed all the prophets with the sword. So Jezebel sent a messenger to Elijah to say, "May the gods deal with me, be it ever so severely, if by this time tomorrow I do not make your life like that of one of them."

Elijah was afraid and ran for his life. When he came to Beersheba in Judah, he left his servant there, while he himself went a day's journey into the wilderness. He came to a broom bush, sat down under it, and prayed that he might die. "I have had enough, Lord," he said. "Take my life; I am no better than my ancestors." Then he lay down under the bush and fell asleep.

All at once an angel touched him and said, "Get up and eat." He looked around, and there by his head was some bread baked over hot coals, and a jar of water. He ate and drank and then lay down again. The angel of the Lord came back a second time and touched him and said, "Get up and eat, for the journey is too much for you." So he got up and ate and drank. Strengthened by that food, he traveled forty days and forty nights until he reached Horeb, the mountain of God.

There he went into a cave and spent the night. And the word of the Lord came to him: "What are you doing here, Elijah?" He replied, "I have been very zealous for the Lord God Almighty. The Israelites have rejected your covenant, torn down your altars, and put your prophets to death with the sword. I am the only one left, and now they are trying to kill me too."

The Lord said, "Go out and stand on the mountain in the presence of the Lord, for the Lord is about to pass by." Then a great and powerful wind tore the mountains apart and shattered the rocks before the Lord, but the Lord was not in the wind. After the wind there was an earthquake, but the Lord was not in the earthquake.

After the earthquake came a fire, but the Lord was not in the fire. And after the fire came a gentle whisper. When Elijah heard it, he pulled his cloak over his face and went out and stood at the mouth of the cave. Then a voice said to him, "What are you doing here, Elijah?"

He replied, "I have been very zealous for the Lord God Almighty. The Israelites have rejected your covenant, torn down your altars, and put your prophets to death with the sword. I am the only one left, and now they are trying to kill me too."

The Lord said to him, "Go back the way you came, and go to the Desert of Damascus. When you get there, anoint Hazael king over Aram. Also, anoint Jehu son of Nimshi king over Israel, and anoint Elisha son of Shaphat from Abel Meholah to succeed you as prophet. [17] Jehu will put to death any who escape the sword of Hazael, and Elisha will put to death any who escape the sword of Jehu. Yet I reserve seven thousand in Israel—all whose knees have not bowed down to Baal and whose mouths have not kissed him."

So Elijah went from there and found Elisha son of Shaphat. He was plowing with twelve yoke of oxen, and he himself was driving the twelfth pair. Elijah went up to him and threw his cloak around him. Elisha then left his oxen and ran after Elijah. "Let me kiss my father and mother goodbye," he said, "and then I will come with you."

"Go back," Elijah replied. "What have I done to you?"

So Elisha left him and went back. He took his yoke of oxen and slaughtered them. He burned the plowing equipment to cook the meat and gave it to the people, and they ate. Then he set out to follow Elijah and became his servant. (1 Kings 19:1–21)

To properly understand the events in chapter 19, it is important to understand what took place in chapters 17–18. In chapter 18, God set the scene for a struggle between his prophet Elijah and King Ahab of Israel. In chapter 17, Elijah had prophesied that a drought would be felt in all the land for the next few years and would not end except at his word. Just as Elijah had prophesied, a drought took place, and King Ahab was furious with Elijah. The king had his men looking for the prophet but could not locate him due to God giving Elijah instructions where to hide.

In chapter 18, spiritual warfare was declared as God instructed Elijah to come out of hiding and present himself to King Ahab. Elijah followed through on God's instructions and went further to use this as an opportunity to turn the people of Israel away from idol worship through the prophets of Baal and back to the Lord. He asked King Ahab to gather all of Israel and the prophets of Baal to Mount Carmel. He issued a challenge to prove that the Lord was the true God, not Baal, by asking for a sacrifice of two bullocks (one for Elijah and one for the prophets of Baal) to be prepared. No fire would be set as the prophets of Baal would call on their god, and Elijah would call on the Lord. The one who answered by providing fire to burn up the sacrifice will be considered God.

The spiritual battle commenced, and though there were over four hundred prophets of Baal calling on their god, nothing happened to their sacrifice. However, when Elijah called on the Lord, his sacrifice was completely incinerated by fire. When the people of Israel witnessed these events, they reaffirmed their commitment to the Lord by lying prostrate on their faces. Afterward, Elijah commanded the people of Israel to execute the prophets of Baal, and the people carried out his orders. Afterward, Elijah prayed for rain, and the Lord brought rain upon the land.

Against this backdrop, we move into the events of chapter 19, which are the subject of our focus for overcoming a faith crisis. Elijah had just experienced an incredible spiritual high, but as is often the case for Christians, that is when Satan decides to take his shots at us. Elijah would not be an exception to this rule. King Ahab whined to his wife, Jezebel, about what Elijah had done to the prophets of

Baal. Jezebel was much more ruthless than her husband, so she sent a message to Elijah letting him know that the next day, she would have him executed just as he had done to the prophets of Baal.

Elijah is considered a spiritual giant, and his entire story makes him deserving of the high regard that the church holds him in today. However, his response to Jezebel's threat was fear, not faith. The text tells us that when he read Jezebel's message, he feared for his life and immediately ran away. Simply put, the man of God had a faith crisis. Unfortunately, many people who profess to be Christians today judge other Christians when they have a faith crisis. Thankfully, God does not function the way we do because he understands that every Christian has a breaking point, so he extends his grace and mercy to us. This brings me to the first step in overcoming a faith crisis, which is that you must acknowledge that you are having a faith crisis. Once you can name what you are dealing with and understand that you are not the first, nor will you be the last, to deal with it, then you are much better positioned to overcome your faith crisis.

The thing that makes a faith crisis so potentially dangerous is that when Christians go through it, Satan really begins working overtime on making us feel both guilty and unworthy of God's love. As we internalize those feelings, we tend to isolate ourselves from God and the people of God. At this point, Satan has us exactly where he wants us because if we are no longer seeking God nor fellowship with the people of God, then it's almost impossible for us to overcome our faith crisis. Also, for some people, the isolation and guilt can lead them to take a permanent solution such as suicide to a temporary problem. For this reason, it is crucial that we understand when we are having a faith crisis, the nature of the faith crisis, and how to navigate through it.

The second step in overcoming a faith crisis is bringing our situation and all its details before God. In our text, Elijah reached out to God after he fled. Unfortunately, it is not a prayer that one would expect from anyone, and certainly not from this legendary man of God. In fact, I will call it a prayer only because, at its basic level, prayer simply means having a conversation with God. However, it's the substance of this conversation that is so troubling because Elijah asked the Lord to take his life, and the reason for why he felt he deserved to die was because "he was no better than his fathers." In other words, Elijah felt guilty and unworthy because he had a faith crisis and for the way he handled it, which made him just like his forefathers who had been unfaithful to God.

Elijah's response to his faith crisis is extreme, but it shows just how dangerous a faith crisis can be if we don't recognize it and deal with it. One of the greatest things about being a child of God is that God's reaction to our crying out to him is always based on love regardless of the circumstances. In Elijah's case, God asked him why he left his home. At this point, it's important to remember that God is omnipotent (all powerful), omnipresent (everywhere), and omniscient (all knowing), which means God is fully aware of what Elijah had done and why he had taken this drastic step along with the feelings he had about his actions. As a result, God asking Elijah a question is not about God needing information; it's about helping Elijah realize the root of his fear and flight. Simply put, God was engaging Elijah in a get-real moment where Elijah was forced to confront his fear and bring it before God. It's only when we get real with God about our failures, fears, anxiety, or issues that God can step in because we are finally ready to allow him to step in.

Elijah did not fully understand the intervention that God had begun in his behalf, but he was fully transparent with God at this point with his response:

> He replied, "I have been very zealous for the Lord God Almighty. The Israelites have rejected your covenant, torn down your altars, and put your prophets to death with the sword. I am the only one left, and now they are trying to kill me too."
> (1 Kings 19:10)

Elijah's response tells us that the root cause of his faith crisis was that he thought he was all by himself when it came to standing for the Lord. This brings me to the third point in overcoming a faith crisis, which is that you are not alone. You and God constitute a majority.

God has all power in his hands; therefore, regardless of how dire our circumstances may seem, God has the power to fix them. The issue is, we must get to a point in our relationship with God that we know this is true for ourselves. Unfortunately, the only way to learn to trust God is to allow him to bring you through a situation, and when you come out on the other side, you know it was only because of God.

God showed up for Elijah during his faith crisis not just with words but by giving him a plan of action.

> He replied, "I have been very zealous for the Lord God Almighty. The Israelites have rejected your covenant, torn down your altars, and put your prophets to death with the sword. I am the only one left, and now they are trying to kill me too."
>
> The Lord said to him, "Go back the way you came, and go to the Desert of Damascus. When you get there, anoint Hazael king over Aram. Also, anoint Jehu son of Nimshi king over Israel, and anoint Elisha son of Shaphat from Abel Meholah to succeed you as prophet. Jehu will put to death any who escape the sword of Hazael, and Elisha will put to death any who escape the sword of Jehu. Yet I reserve seven thousand in Israel—all whose knees have not bowed down to Baal and whose mouths have not kissed him." (1 Kings 19:14–18)

God's action plan was designed to prove to Elijah that God was going to address all his concerns. First, he told Elijah to anoint replacements for the king of Haram (Hazael) and the king of Israel (Jehu). By having Elijah anoint these successors, God was letting him know that he was sovereign over the entire world, including who he will allow to serve as kings.

Step one of the action plan addressed Elijah's fear of Jezebel because God was promising to take Ahab and Jezebel's power and give it to someone who would acknowledge and serve God. Second, he told Elijah to anoint Elisha as his successor. Anointing Elisha provided Elijah with the comfort of knowing that he would have direct support in his ministry efforts; this also let him know that the work of God would continue long after he was off the scene. Finally, God told Elijah that he had seven thousand people in Israel who had never worshipped idols. This part of the battle plan was to help Elijah understand that there were many people in Israel who loved and worshipped God just as Elijah did.

The final point in overcoming a faith crisis is that we must stand on the promises of God. In Elijah's case, it meant he had to trust God to bring to pass everything that he had told him regarding the plan of action. Elijah was redeemed and ready to go forth in ministry because of the comfort and encouragement that God had given him.

Overcoming a faith crisis is not just for spiritual giants like Elijah; rather, it is for *all* members of God's family. Life is hard, and we must be able to endure the good and bad things that will occur. However, it becomes easier to navigate these things when you never lose sight of the fact that you are a child of God, and he has promised to protect and provide for you as you stand for him.

CHAPTER 10

Life Is Better When We Do It Together

One of the most overlooked aspects of Christianity is the importance of fellowship. I have heard many people say over the years some version of the following statement, "I don't need to go to church because I can worship God by myself at home." It is true that we can worship God whenever and wherever we are; we are free to worship him by ourselves as well. In fact, I will go further and say that we should have a time where we worship God by ourselves because that is our quality time with him, which allows us to grow closer to him. However, if our worship never includes other believers, then we are missing a very important aspect of Christianity.

Fellowship is important to God, and he models it for us in scripture. In the book of Genesis, when God began to create mankind, it says, "Let us make man in our own image." The *Us* is referring to the Triune God of God the Father, God the Son, and God the Holy Spirit. In the very beginning, God is keying us in the reality that the Triune God exists in perfect harmony and fellowship. Each part of the Triune God has different responsibilities, but they all make up the Triune God.

For readers who consider themselves only needing to adhere to the New Testament, let's look at 1 John 5:7, which says, "For these three-bear witness in heaven, the Father, the Word, and the Holy Spirit and these three are one." This is the same idea that was emphasized in Genesis but is merely being restated in the

New Testament. This concept of unity, harmony, and fellowship is frequently expressed in Scripture because God knows the importance of us being accountable to one another and strengthening one another.

We are certainly free to worship God by ourselves and should take full advantage of the opportunity to do so, but that does not mean we should exclude ourselves from fellowship. In fact, scripture commands us to fellowship.

> And let us consider how we may spur one another on toward love and good deeds, not giving up meeting together, as some are in the habit of doing, but encouraging one another—and all the more as you see the Day approaching. (Hebrews 10:24–25)

Hebrews 10:24–25 places a premium on Christians coming together; or in today's vernacular, we would say coming to church. The text conveys three important points: First, fellowship is an expression of love. As Christians, everything we do is supposed to be rooted in love. When we come together in fellowship, it expresses our love and value for one another. Unfortunately, merely showing up to the church building is not genuine fellowship if your heart and motives for being there are not pure.

During my undergraduate years at the Ohio State University, I was blessed to meet a young lady named Lynnette Cosby (Valentine at that time). She was born and raised in Columbus, Ohio, and an active member of Friendship Baptist Church in Columbus, Ohio. My friends and I routinely went to church with her every Sunday. I enjoyed going to church as I always had done, but at that stage of my life, I wasn't ready to change any of my sinful ways. I attended church every week, but very little spiritual growth took place for me during those five years. I simply wasn't ready to fully embrace God yet, and I certainly hadn't reached a point where my actions were motivated by love. Thankfully, the Lord wasn't finished with me yet. Once I made the decision after graduating from college of moving back home to

Cleveland, I was truly ready to embrace fellowship in its truest biblical sense, and my life has been different since that time.

Second, fellowship requires us to encourage one another. One of Satan's best weapons against Christians is to isolate us from our support systems. Many Christians, especially men, have vilified Eve for her actions in the Garden of Eden, for eating the forbidden fruit and persuading her husband to do the same. Patriarchal worldviews have used the story to falsely assert that women are weak. However, the reality is that men and women are equally vulnerable to Satan's attack when we are isolated from our support system. Sadly enough, the same saints who vilify Eve do not acknowledge that the text lets us know that Adam was present for the encounter, but he sat there quietly and allowed Eve to fall prey to Satan. When she needed her husband the most, his silence was not only akin to isolation but also spiritual abandonment. If Satan had approached Adam first, the results would have likely been the same as with Eve.

Finally, fellowship puts us in a proper mindset to be ready to receive Jesus when he returns. When Jesus was asked which commandment is the greatest, he replied that we should love the Lord with all our heart, mind, and strength and love our neighbor as ourselves. It is impossible to fulfill the commitment toward our neighbor without embracing genuine fellowship.

Fellowship is part of God's redemptive plan, and when we reject it, we are rejecting his plan. As a person who has been guilty of rejecting God's plan for my life on many different occasions, I fully understand the consequences of this rejection. I have learned to embrace fellowship, and I can say with no hesitation that it allows you to see things differently.

Church can be a confusing place sometimes because, on a basic level, a church is like hospital in the sense that everyone is dealing with some type of issue. Plenty of people have experienced deep pain in church, which makes it difficult for them to want to come to church; or if they come, they refuse to actively engage. Once you actively engage, you open yourself up to the possibly of being hurt.

I understand all these points because I have been there, done that, and have the T-shirt when it comes to experiencing hurt in church. However, the thing that has helped me the most in overcoming the pain is understanding that God is my salvation and is not part of pain. When I embrace fellowship, I open myself up to a deeper relationship with God as well as the people around me. Engaging with the people around us, we can learn from one another's pain, support one another, encourage one another, and love one another. If we can do those things for one another, then we can simply trust God to do the things we can't do.

About the Author

Melvin Davis is a lifelong resident of the Greater Cleveland, Ohio, area where he lives with his wife, Alisha, and their nine-year-old daughter, Kayla. Melvin has three adult children (Carmalicia, Shaquille, and Tashara). Melvin is a graduate of the Ohio State University, where he received a BA in political science; University of Akron, where he received a juris doctor; and Ashland Theological Seminary, where he received a master of arts in practical theology. Melvin served in the Navy Reserves for eight years, including a fifteen-month deployment to Iraq. Melvin is an ordained minister and is currently a member of New Community Bible Fellowship in Cleveland Heights, Ohio, where he serves as an adult student leader in the church's student ministry for teens.

www.ingramcontent.com/pod-product-compliance
Lightning Source LLC
Chambersburg PA
CBHW022118150726
47990CB00003B/1414